Pioneer Children
of Appalachia
by Joan Anderson
Photographs by George Ancona

Clarion Books
Ticknor & Fields · New York

To my father, who taught me his survival skills   –J.A.

To Maxine B. Rosenberg   –G.A.

Clarion Books
Ticknor & Fields, a Houghton Mifflin Company
Text copyright © 1986 by Joan Anderson
Photographs copyright © 1986 by George Ancona

Library of Congress Cataloging-in-Publication Data
Anderson, Joan. Pioneer children of Appalachia.
Summary: Text and photographs from a living history
village in West Virginia re-create the pioneer life of
young people in Appalachia in the early nineteenth
century.
1. Pioneer children—West Virginia—Juvenile
literature. 2. Pioneer children—Appalachian Region,
Southern—Juvenile literature. 3. West Virginia—
Social life and customs—Juvenile literature.
4. Appalachian Region, Southern—Social life and
customs—Juvenile literature. 5. Frontier and pioneer
life—West Virginia—Juvenile literature. 6. Frontier
and pioneer life—Appalachian Region, Southern—Juvenile
literature. [1. Frontier and pioneer life—Appalachian
Region. 2. Appalachian Region—Social life and customs.
3. West Virginia—Social life and customs] I. Ancona,
George, ill. II. Title.
F241.A58   1986   975.4′57   86-2624
ISBN 0-89919-440-0

HO   10   9   8   7   6   5   4   3   2   1

Introduction

Between 1790 and 1830, hundreds of Americans moved into the rugged hills and narrow hollows, or hollers, of what became the state of West Virginia. In those days long before supermarkets, factories, and cars, a pioneer family made almost everything it needed to survive. Children worked as hard as their parents and grandparents did.

This book re-creates the life-style of the fictional Davis family. The scenes were photographed at Fort New Salem in Salem, West Virginia, a living history museum celebrating the folkways of Appalachia. The museum, which is part of nearby Salem College, carefully preserves and teaches the traditional survival crafts of the pioneers.

Elizabeth remembered the lonely look on Ma's face as they said good-bye. Ma was expecting a baby, and everyone hoped it would arrive before the cold weather did.

Aunt Jane had come to the Davis cabin to help take care of things. Even so, Elizabeth and Isaac had done chores before starting out. Isaac helped Pa sharpen the axes to chop down trees at Grandpa's.

Elizabeth milked Bossie and fed the chickens. Next she gathered ashes from the hearth to fill the wooden hopper used for soapmaking. Then she placed a bucket under the hopper's spout to catch the water she poured through.

After Elizabeth had soaked the ashes and let the water drip through ten or more times, the bucket was full of lye water. This strong solution was mixed with fat to make soap.

While Elizabeth was away, Ma and Aunt Jane would finish the job. They would boil the lye in a big kettle with beef tallow. The smell was always horrible! Elizabeth was glad she could leave before that part of the process.

Ma and Aunt Jane would stir the mixture until it thickened. Then they would pour it into gourds and old dishes, leaving it to semi-harden. Afterward, they would cut it into cakes and leave them to harden in the sun.

There sure would be plenty of soap
for the laundry days ahead, Elizabeth
thought.

Just after the Davises crossed Indian Run Creek, Isaac spotted something.

"Hey, Pa, look over there," he whispered. "A rabbit—good size, too."

Pa took quick aim with his flintlock and fired. The sound echoed wildly through the woods.

"You got 'im, Pa," Isaac yelled as he scampered off to retrieve their prize. He picked it up and started to run ahead, the dead rabbit dangling from his hand. Elizabeth hurried to catch up.

They finally arrived at Raccoon Run and the beginning of Big Flint. That was the name of Grandpa's land. Each family's property was named after the owner or after the nearest stream. Flint Billy was Grandpa's nickname.

"There's the cabin!" Elizabeth shouted.

Grandma and Grandpa were waiting on the porch. Elizabeth planted a kiss on Grandpa's cheek. Isaac followed his nose to Grandma's gingerbread, baking in the hearth.

But Pa announced that they should save the fun for suppertime. "We have to use what little daylight is left to find trees for Grandpa's baskets. C'mon, Isaac, grab your ax."

Pa and Isaac headed over the hill to where the best white oaks were growing. Grandpa called after them, "Make sure you find trees without knots! And remember, they should be straight as arrows."

Pa nodded and smiled. He was amused that after all these years Grandpa still thought only *he* knew which trees made good baskets.

They found several white oaks and began chopping. Dusk was creeping up on them as the sixth tree tumbled over.

"It's near dark, my boy," Pa said. "Grab ahold of that there small tree. I'll take this one. We'll come back in the morning for the others."

Elizabeth had spent a restful afternoon talking with Grandma as they strung sliced apples. Stringing fruits and vegetables was a way to preserve food. The garlands were hung out in the sunlight to dry. Then they were brought back inside to hang near the hearth until they were needed for a meal.

As they worked, Grandma told again the story of the Davis clan's journey from New Jersey to "north Western Virginny." Sometimes Elizabeth wished her family would move on farther west. But Grandma's tales of hardship on the trail made her grateful for the settled life she had been born into at Crooked Run.

Early the next morning, when Grandma wasn't looking, Elizabeth slipped out of the cabin to gather plants for Grandma's special remedies. Grandma should know how I've learned right well the different plants, barks, and berries, Elizabeth thought to herself.

Not far from the cabin, Elizabeth spotted a field of goldenrod and Joe-Pye weed. Farther on she found cherry bark and sassafras root. Soon her basket was overflowing.

SASSAFRAS ROOT
for spring tonic

GARLIC
for colds

COLTSFOOT
for chest colds

YARROW
for fever

POKEBERRY
for arthritis

CHERRY BARK
for cough syrup

Elizabeth knew Grandma Davis was the smartest person around when it came to making folks well. Grandma insisted that the good Lord wouldn't have wasted his time creating plants, or yarbs as she called them, if they weren't for some use. "It's up to us humans to figure out what they are for," Grandma always said.

Back at the cabin, Grandma had been looking all over for Elizabeth. But when she saw the brimming basket, Grandma broke into a big smile. Together they sorted the plants and tied them into bunches to dry in the shed behind the cabin. Then Grandma brewed a pot of special tea that was "good for the constitution." She poured a cup for Elizabeth.

Meanwhile, the men had gathered by the shed to split the fresh wood. Grandpa was directing, but Pa was doing much of the heavy work.

First, they split the logs, using iron wedges. "I shouldn't be stoopin' over so much," Grandpa said. "Blood rushes to my head and makes me dizzy."

Then, with a tool called a froe, they split the wood into thinner pieces. Next, Grandpa sat on the shaving horse. He removed the bark and shaved each piece evenly with a drawknife. "With you all doing the heavy work," he said, "I may just get caught up on my orders. Them there baskets take four days to make. When ya think about it, making a basket from a tree is somewhat of a miracle."

Next Grandpa split the pieces evenly until he had narrow strips. Finally, he shaved thin strips that would become the flexible splints for his baskets.

Now Grandpa nailed several splints to a board to form the bottom of the basket and to make a frame around which he could weave the sides.

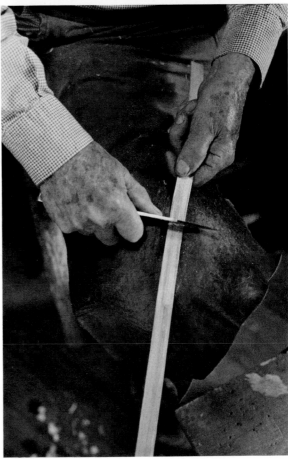

"C'mon over, Elizabeth," Grandpa said, "and put your finger right here. Now hold tight while I get a couple of splints a-goin'. Time was when my fingers worked in ten different directions. Not so anymore." Grandpa sounded so sad that Elizabeth was doubly glad she was there to help.

A sturdy basket was an everyday necessity for a woman. It was practically an extension of her arm as she gathered eggs, carried food to the neighbors, or performed a dozen other tasks.

By late afternoon, Pa figured they had accomplished so much that he announced, "We best be heading home to Ma. If we hurry, we'll see Crooked Run 'fore dark."

It was almost pitch-black when the Davises sniffed the friendly smell of smoke from the cabin chimney drifting on the night air. The candlelit windows guided them to the cabin door, and Elizabeth and Isaac headed straight to their beds in the loft.

The next morning Pa, like always, hit the broomstick on the cabin ceiling to rattle Elizabeth and Isaac out of their beds. Reluctantly, they climbed down into the one-room cabin. Life at Crooked Run was back to normal—everyone working from sunup to sunset.

"Aunt Jane here's been up since 'fore dawn," Pa said, "doin' your chores, Elizabeth. This ain't no special day. Our trip to Grandpa is behind us. But since Bossie's been milked and the chickens fed, the day should feel special to you."

Pa winked as he finished his tirade. Elizabeth knew he wasn't really angry at her for sleeping late. After a hearty breakfast, she headed out to the yard to the jobs awaiting her.

Aunt Jane had filled the kettle with beef tallow that was melting over the hot flames. "Looks like we do the candle-dippin' first," Elizabeth said to Isaac. He gave her a disagreeable look, wishing for any other job. But the truth was that if they didn't make candles now, it would be a very dark winter. As they approached the kettle, Elizabeth held her nose in disgust at the rancid smell of the melting fat.

She and Isaac attached several wicks to a piece of wood so they could dip a number of candles at once. They had a competition to see who could make the thickest candles in the shortest time. Each candle had to be dipped at least twenty-five times, and dipping needed just the right touch. If the candles were in the hot wax more than a second, they would never build up because the wax from the previous dip would melt!

Today's job took them way past noon. But they had 120 candles to show for it.

After cleaning up the mess, Elizabeth was sent off to pull flax. The Davis family had a good crop this year. That meant Ma and Elizabeth could make lots of linen during the long winter days.

First, Elizabeth spent several hours carefully pulling the flax plant out of the ground by the root.

Then she tied the flax into bunches. For the next few days the flax would go through a dew-retting process—the morning and evening dew would soften the stems.

When Pa thought the flax was ready, he and Elizabeth would pull the dew-retted stems through a device called a hackle until the flax was in condition to be spun.

When all the flax had gone through the hackle, Ma could begin to spin it into thread. It would take weeks of spinning before Ma had enough to weave cloth. Then she would wait until Jud Smith came by with his loom.

What a treat it was to have new dresses, shirts, and pants! Mountain folk had only one change of clothes because it took so long to make cloth. Even when clothing wore out, the scraps were used for quilts and baby clothes. Nothing was ever discarded.

Meanwhile, Isaac was helping Pa hollow out a sycamore stump they had found in the woods. The stump would be made into a storage bin for food staples such as beans, peas, and corn.

First, Isaac collected dry oak shavings and stuffed them into the stump. Then Pa lit a fire inside, the flames shooting out like a big explosion.

Next Pa kicked the stump on its side and rolled it about the ground so that the entire inside would be softened. After the fire died down, Pa and Isaac would take turns scraping out the insides of the stump until it was a good size for storing food. Then they would make a tight cover to keep wild creatures out and the food safe inside.

A few days later Pa took Elizabeth and Isaac off to the town of New Salem to do errands. Although the Davises made all they could for themselves, certain items still had to be purchased. Money was almost nonexistent, so the Davis family would barter—exchange labor or goods—for what they needed.

Today Pa wanted Isaac to get nails for the new shed they were building. Isaac worked the bellows in the blacksmith's shop in return for the nails. Meanwhile, Elizabeth traded eggs and smoked pork with the townspeople for sugar and salt.

While the children were about their business, Pa paid a visit to the tavern. This was a general meeting place for men from surrounding parts. Here they could exchange local political news and pick up the mail, which was delivered to the tavern by a rider on horseback. Pa got a letter from his brother, Uncle Matthew, who had relocated a little farther north.

To Elizabeth's delight, Ely George, the itinerant peddler, was in town. He carried all sorts of treasures from the big city. The machine-made trinkets were her favorites, and Ely loved showing her his newest wares.

On the walk home, the children told Pa everything they had seen and heard. Elizabeth thought that life for New Salem folk sure looked easy compared with life in the holler.

Soon the days began to grow shorter, and cornfields in the hollers were begging to be harvested. Word went out that a workin', or harvesting, was planned for Saturday.

On Saturday morning, Pa and Isaac set out early to join the other harvesters at the Jacksons'. When that field was cleared, everyone would move on over to the Wilsons', then to Crooked Run, and finally end up at Grandpa's field. There the children would be waiting to play in the corn shock tepees. Harvest time was work *and* play for men, women, and children alike.

Several of Ma's friends stopped by to take Elizabeth to the harvest festival because Ma couldn't go this year. They carried along freshly slaughtered chickens and wild game, eggs, flour, sugar, apples, berries—anything that would make a grand supper following the workin'.

In Grandma's kitchen, the women sang "Barbara Allen" and other favorite tunes as they pared apples to make apple butter, chopped vegetables for rabbit stew, prepared squirrel meat for frying, and whipped up bowls of corn mush. Once the meal preparations were well under control, the ladies and girls moved into Grandma's living room for a quiltin'.

They had started the quilt last winter as a gift for bride-to-be Rebecca Randolph.

"She's a special one," Grandma kept repeating. "Is there anyone who works harder tendin' to the sick?"

Usually Elizabeth was allowed to do some quilting, but this one was too special for her inexperienced hands. Nevertheless, she loved listening to the conversation of the grown-ups. She also wondered who would catch the cat.

When a quilt for a bride was completed, a cat was placed in the center. The quilt was tossed up and down until the cat flew into someone's arms. The woman or girl who caught it was supposed to be married next. Elizabeth looked around at the unmarried ladies. She wished Aunt Jane could be there when the quilt was tossed. She'd make some man a fine wife.

Just then the men arrived. The workin' was over, and they were ready to eat. But Pa called out, "Whoa, wait a minute, you young'ns. No feasting till the job is all done. Out by the shed is a mighty big pile of corn to be husked!"

With their stomachs growling, the young people sat in a circle and shucked as fast as they could. There was laughter and talk and general fun, especially when Ruth Wilson discovered that she was shucking the only red ear of corn. The young man or woman with the red ear got to kiss the person of his or her choice. Ruth held up the ear with a mischievous grin and gazed at Benjamin Evans.

Just as they started to kiss, someone clanged a pot from the kitchen announcing that supper was served.

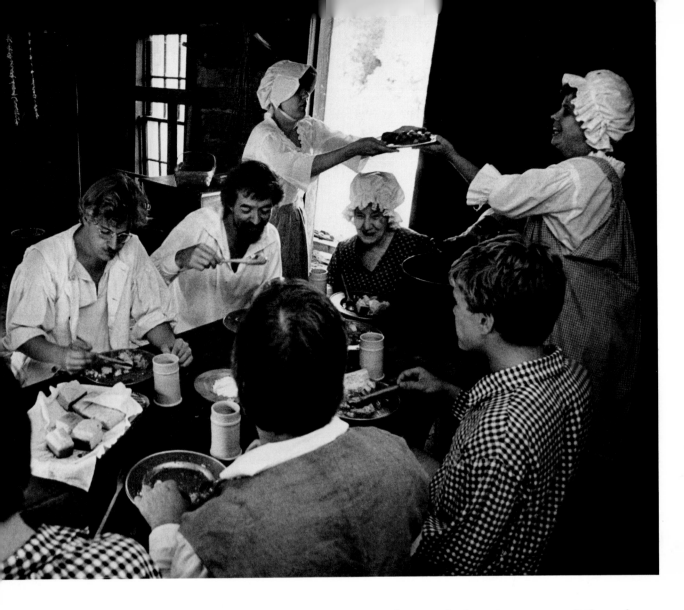

As usual, there were two sittings for the feast. During "first table," the men ate alone, served by the women. During "second table," the women and children ate together. Grandma, as the hostess, stayed at the table for both servings.

After everyone had feasted, Ely George took out his fiddle to play some good dancing music. In no time at all, there were two full squares of couples.

Some folks danced, while others sang, clapped their hands, or tapped their feet.

Elizabeth, Isaac, and the other children were too young for the dancing, so the women entertained them by helping them make corn husk dolls and corn husk fiddles with scraps left from the shucking.

Elizabeth soaked the husks in water so she could bend them any way she wanted. Then one of the women helped her shape a doll she could use as a bookmark for her Bible. Elizabeth draped a cape around the doll's shoulders and made long hair for her with corn silk.

Isaac tried to squeak out a tune on his new corn husk fiddle. One thing was for certain—a workin' was fun for everyone!

Now that the harvest was over, Elizabeth knew winter was on the way. Few noises would break the winter stillness at Crooked Run—just the cries of the newborn baby, Ma's gentle lullabies, or Pa's gunfire when he was lucky enough to find a deer.

The cold wind would swirl around the cabin, meaning no harm to the occupants inside. The sturdy little house at Crooked Run would keep the Davises secure and cozy the whole winter through.

Pa had followed Grandpa's advice: "Prepare for the worst, expect the best, and then take whatever comes." Now Elizabeth and her family could take a welcome rest from the toil of mountain life until the first signs of spring appeared outside the cabin door.

Our Thanks

During the time we were working on this book at Fort New Salem, we experienced "country"—a life-style that is chock-full of warmth, hospitality, down-home values, and mountain pride. We are extremely grateful to John Randolph, who founded and directs Fort New Salem, thereby enabling folks like us to know and feel the true character of Appalachia. We also thank Noel Tenney, Co-ordinator of Museum Education, for his hospitality on two separate occasions and for helping to make this book historically accurate.

We are especially grateful to George Pinkham, who played Pa. He created the spirit of the fictional Davis family, and without him we would not have had the wonderful location shots and special props. To the other interpreters—Sandy Godfrey, Amy Jo Pinkham, and Charlie Underwood, who completed the Davis family; Ireta Randolph, Fred Means, Shelba Zirkle, Connie Serrell, and little Jonathan Pinkham—we express our gratitude for their patience during the long hours of work. Much appreciation also goes to Paula Batson for the use of her farm and to Duke and Lillian Pinkham for their noonday meal and modern-day West Virginian hospitality.

Closer to home, we thank Jim Giblin and Ann Troy for their inspiration and painstaking interest in this project, and Adelia Geiger for getting the author to Fort New Salem on her first visit.

Joan Anderson & George Ancona